Herbert Howells
Three Psalm Preludes for Organ

Set two

Cover drawing by BRENDA MOORE, reproduced by permission of
the Royal College of Music.

NOVELLO PUBLISHING LIMITED
8/9 Frith Street, London W1V 5TZ

Order No: NOV 590355

PSALM-PRELUDES
(SECOND SET)
I
For John Dykes Bower

De profundis clamavi
ad te, Domine
Ps. 130: v.1

Herbert Howells

I Ch.
II Gt
III Sw.

Lento, dolente (♪ = 62)

(to III) 8′ only

2

estinto   un poco più mosso (♪ = 76)

ten.

poco sonore

un poch. agitato e poco a poco
accel.

7

lunga

più lento, assai tranquillo

molto lento

(H.H. London. 29-9-1938)

PSALM - PRELUDES
(SECOND SET)
II

For William H. Harris

"Yea, the darkness is no darkness
with Thee, but the night is as
clear as the day: the darkness
and light to Thee are both
alike."

Ps. 139 : v. 11

I Ch.
II G!
III Sw.

Herbert Howells

estinto

un pochettino più movimento
sempre con anima

mp I–III

più

H.H. London. 12. IV 1939

PSALM-PRELUDES

(SECOND SET)

III

For Percy C. Hull

"Sing unto Him a new song:
play skilfully with a loud noise."
Ps. 33: v. 3

Herbert Howells

I Ch.
II Gt.
III Sw.

16

cresc.

Tuba

sff

III (Full)

p

marc.

to III

II

II

to II

a poco a poco slentando

III

III

sempre dim.

to III
(II to Ped. off)

più animato
(Tempo I)

ancora più animato, ed accel. a poco a poco ($\quarternote$ = 138)

[allarg. - -]

ancora accel.

H. H. London. 27-6-1939

9/94 (18754)